HEART
TO HANDS

HEART
TO HANDS

MAKING YOUR COMMUNITY STRONGER
THROUGH HEARTFELT INTENTION
AND POWERFUL ACTIONS

Kathleen Frantz

WINDY CITY
PUBLISHERS

HEART to HANDS

Windy City Publishers
2118 Plum Grove Road, #349
Rolling Meadows, IL 60008
windycitypublishers.com

Published in the United States of America

ISBN:
978-1-941478-71-4

Library of Congress Control Number:
2018951077

WINDY CITY PUBLISHERS
CHICAGO

I dedicate *Heart To Hands*
to every person who has touched my life so far
and every person who will touch my life in meaningful ways
in the years to come.

To my family, my friends, and one of the dearest
and most influential persons
to impact my life, Carole Magnusson.
Carole taught me perspective, how to let go, how to be present,
and most of all, why it is **equally** important to receive as to give.

Contents

PREFACE

Heart *To Hands* is a reminder of the power that each individual carries in everyday life. You yourself are an expert on your life; these stories and experiences will offer tremendous insight in how you choose to share your expertise to make a difference. We humans are endowed with our own individual talents and gifts, each unique.

When we decide to share our gifts with others, that decision can spread in ways we may not see. This act helps us participate in the unification of our community. Sharing our gifts with other people contributes to the spread of happiness and openness, hopefully touching everyone around us.

Each community I interviewed for the book, I asked: "Can you list the top ten ways people can help in your community that doesn't involve direct donations of funds?" Some of the suggestions were universal, but they also had several ideas unique to them. I loved the inspiring stories I asked them to share. Many of the heartwarming stories displayed how a person's small action led the way to creating a powerful impact in their community. These impacts ranged from affecting one person to an entire community. As I listened to the stories shared, I found myself filled with utter joy and inspiration.

Recently, as I was working through a challenging time, I shared it with a friend. She compared me to a tree. I asked, "What do you mean?" She explained, "Like a tree, you can weather a storm, bend in the storm, and still not break."

I was a little confused, but intrigued. This sparked my curiosity and I decided to look further into trees and their attributes. As I learned more, it occurred to me that trees can be a great example of how we can participate in life. To me, a tree is strength, flexibility, ever giving (all shapes and sizes), sustainable, deeply rooted into its surroundings, and doesn't compete with other trees to stand tall. Remarkably, trees don't compete to grow. Instead, they adapt to their surroundings, allowing the trees in the area to flourish amongst one another.

Fundamentally, trees are the same, yet, different from each other. Their differences may be due in part to their environment, age, stability or type. A tree doesn't worry if it is making the most of the available resources, such as the sun, air, and water. Therefore, a tree is better equipped to care for its surroundings. When a tree is thriving, it provides shade, a home or nourishment for animals, and it filters the air of impurities. These traits make a difference in its surroundings.

SHARING YOUR GIFTS SPREADS JOY.

This inspired me to draw the tree on the cover of the book. The unique hearts represent love and talent available to give and receive, so we can all flourish. At times, we experience forces that seem greater than ourselves, but we can stand strong. Like a tree in a storm, our challenge will pass and we can get back to growing and strengthening ourselves. We can then be there for family, community, and those we care for. You can be the nurturing tree when you decide to share your gifts with others. Your nurturing can provide help to people when they need it and in turn, help bring communities closer. Sharing your gifts spreads joy.

In 2017, I experienced the eclipse of the sun. It would have been great to see the total eclipse, but where I was, in a town just outside of the totality, I could experience 99.9 percent of the eclipse and avoid all the traffic and crowds. Even at 99.9 percent, the little glimmer that was visible was enough to light the world. The total eclipse was being viewed at different times during its passing over the earth. On the NASA channel, we were able to watch the full eclipse before it reached us. The dark of complete totality only lasted a small moment in time before light emerged again. The first reoccurrence of light, the corona with one bright glint, is called the diamond ring effect. How appropriate—the image of a diamond of multifaceted light, generating ever more rays of light. It seemed a call to all of us on this earth to be the light we wish to see in this world, one small spark that sparks another, and another, and another, until the light eclipses the dark.

We are the only ones in charge of our thoughts and actions. At some time in our lives we have all experienced the conflict of being heard by some of the people in our lives and ignored by others. If we are heard we feel reassured and validated; if we are not heard, we feel unappreciated, hurt, and resentful. Something deep in us feels that need to be heard and knows that we would help one another if we had the chance. We should be aware that most people want to be part of a great change.

My hope for this book is that people will understand that now is the time to empower others, even with as simple an act as taking your neighbor's trash to the curb. Every kind deed makes a difference. Let your good intentions flow without expectation of return. Give freely, and something will return filled with love and support, though perhaps not in a way you anticipate. When it does happen, be grateful, and know that all kind actions allow the good in the world to shine and encourage more good to grow.

From this starting place, remember that you are a beautiful being.

LET GO AND RELEASE

Look in the mirror and tell yourself you are worthy of
abundance, love, prosperity, friendships, joy, happiness.
Look directly through your eyes into to your soul.
Really see the beauty in and around you.
Fall in love with your spirit and self.
Be proud and glad that you are one with your spirit.
Hold tight to the positive, let go of the negative;
and most of all—enjoy the ride!

Take your loving intentions in your heart and move them into your hands to bring them to life. This step will help bring the change to empower one another and thus our communities, allowing others to see and follow our actions.

Introduction

E very September, the Charities Aid Foundation releases a World Giving Index; a global view of giving trends. It ranks according to the percent of people helping a stranger, donating money, and volunteering their time. 2017 was the first year every westernized country in the top twenty had a decreased score from the previous year in all three categories. Africa was the only continent to increase in all three. You can review this report through their website cafonline.org under the World Giving Index.

According to Philanthropy Daily and the National Center for Charitable Statistics, the United States has close to 465,000 charitable organizations, including private foundations. They define charitable organizations as "private initiatives, for public good, engaged in public fund-raising for tax-deductible donations." The National Philanthropic Trust charitable giving statistics state: "Americans gave $389.05 billion to charity in 2016." Numbers can vary and reports point to several different aspects outlining what type of groups are contributing and where their contributions are going.

The thing is, whether you look at the news of the decrease in giving or if you look at the large amount of funds that are given in 2016, the environment of giving is changing. When I travel, I have had several conversations with people who say, they just don't know where to start. Perhaps the downward trend is a combination of reasons, but to me, it just means we need to approach it with a fresh eye. In my heart, I believe people want to make a difference in the world, in their country and in their community if they can find the right avenue for them.

Donating money to a charity; for many, it is just not financially feasible. Some believe it doesn't really do anything, and others are "busy" until a personal tragedy may occur in their lives, and then they get involved.

The reason does not really matter. The world keeps changing and needs us to change along with it. Therefore, if charitable donations aren't for you, you can find another way to contribute. What matters is that you are doing something to create the change you are seeking. Who doesn't want to see a world filled with peace, love, and compassion? I would like to say that in our hearts, we all do, even, if we don't know it yet. If you do, it is your time to join in and empower one another.

Can you imagine the change in the world if we all gave back? We could truly be the leader of a "New World." I am not talking about money. Giving is more than money; giving of oneself is genuine, from the heart, and we do not need a dime to be part of the solution. Gifts of the heart can generate life-giving experiences.

GIFTS FROM THE HEART CAN GENERATE LIFE-GIVING EXPERIENCES.

Philanthropic donations, of course, have their place, and many organizations do outstanding work. But they are one part of a greater picture of strengthening our communities.

2

So the question becomes, how do people who donate live or think in a manner that allows them to share what they have so easily? The answer lies in their mindset and how they apply it. They come from a place of abundance, and with an abundant mindset we can achieve anything. Money isn't the definition of abundance; it is only an effect of abundant living. We can look at our gifts, talents, time, love, and other attributes as an abundant source that can help us feel good about sharing and receiving. In the end, sharing your talents can be as effective as donating funds.

It is time to be part of the solution, even if it is simply a smile shared with a sad person. Giving beyond your means is not necessary. What is necessary is redefining what your means are and their significance to you today.

When we think abundantly, we begin to live abundantly, no matter how much money we have, where we live, our age, our race, our creed, or our level of education. If we allow our inner spirit to help guide us during these times of change, it can lead us to live with gratitude. We can become more of what we are grateful for by sharing our abundant talents and gifts. Your simple acts of kindness will open the door for gifts to you in return and help you to continue on your path to be what you believe you can be. These gifts are from the experiences you encounter when sharing. It could be through laughter, a smile, utter joy, or a loving touch from another person, to name a few. These gifts may seem small, but they can be powerful and produced solely through generosity and care for another. It is in the knowing that you have touched each other on a deeper level that these gifts become so powerful; the fact that you took the time to listen, acknowledge, share, and assist.

INTRODUCTION

As a society, it can appear that we continue to rely on social media to form our views and understandings of the world around us. Today, our news comes in fast and fleeting. To add to it, the use of fake media to mislead us is increasingly difficult to decipher. Combine this with people interacting less and less as a community, and we're called to bring change into action. It is easy to learn how to take small steps that are truly impactful. It just takes the desire and the will to change and make a positive difference in our own lives and in the lives of others. It is time to take ownership of the goodness we have inside of us and create a will to use it.

It doesn't take much to make a difference in a person's life. If we think that we have to do it all, it can become overwhelming. The good news is; it is not up to one person. That is why there are so many of us. Let's work together to help inspire one another by going out and sharing small acts of kindness and sharing our good deeds to inspire others to go out and do the same. This will create a larger impact across our communities. As the old saying goes, "Many hands make light work."

IT ALL BEGINS SOMEWHERE...

When I entered first grade after a year of kindergarten, it did not take me long to figure out that if your birthday fell during the school year you were treated with special attention and received some nice privileges. But if your birthday fell during the summer, there were no bells and whistles celebrating your special day.

Our first-grade teacher, Mrs. Parzack, was the teacher every child loved—and for good reason. She made everyone who entered her room feel special. On your birthday, she dialed it up a notch and made your day in class stand out. She adorned you with a beautiful (and personally crafted) construction paper crown. The class sang to you, and you had the honor of bringing the attendance chart down to the office, cleaning the erasers at the end of the day, and many more special activities.

I soon realized that since my birthday fell during summer break, in August, I was not going to have my "special day." I didn't think it was very fair, so I decided to take matters into my own hands. I marched right up to my teacher one morning and boldly stated that today was my birthday. She looked a little confused but went right to her class roster. She looked at my name, looked up from her book with a smile, and apologized for missing my birthday. It would take a minute to complete my crown, and then we would start the day.

She adorned me with the coveted paper crown that I wore all day, the class sang *Happy Birthday*, and I received all the attention I expected. It felt odd, but I was happy I got to celebrate my birthday, like everyone else with a birthday falling during the school year. I had a wonderful day.

I walked home on cloud nine. When I arrived home, my mom asked me why I was wearing the crown. When she heard my story, she made me turn around and walk right back to school to tell my teacher the truth. I was devastated, and the walk back felt like a walk of shame.

When I arrived back at school, Mrs. Parzack was at her desk grading papers. Head down, I slowly walked over and shared the truth and the reason behind my deceit. She listened patiently, the smile never leaving her face. When I finished, she showed me her roster with my actual birthday clearly marked next to my name. She explained that in her eyes no harm would come from allowing me a special day. She expressed her gratitude that I had told the truth and was happy I did so. She gave me a hug and sent me on my way. I felt her love and warmth and left feeling relieved and heard. The walk back was even better than the first time I went home that day.

On the last day of school that year, I stayed after to help clean up. As I was about to leave she presented me with a gift, two copies of a book called *Leo the Late Bloomer* by Robert Kraus. She instructed me to share the extra copy with someone else who might benefit from it. I read this book over and over. I loved it, and I kept the two books close by at all times.

Leo the tiger cub was a late bloomer. He didn't learn to read and write when the other animal children did and he wasn't good at other skills either. His father worried and his mother counseled patience. Leo bloomed when the time was right for him. When he did bloom he was able to write, read, draw, and eat neatly, and he and his parents were happy.

The book gave me hope and inspiration, allowing me to understand that it might take time for me to be able to do or experience things that others already could. At the right time and in my own way I would blossom and become good at things I chose. I held the book, as well as the lessons it taught me, in high regard. I was very conscious of the responsibility of sharing it with someone else.

I realized who would receive my second copy of *Leo the Late Bloomer* roughly ten years later. I could tell that this book would benefit her in the same way that it had empowered me. I continued to hold my book close to my heart and discovered that its meaning changed as my awareness grew. At times I thought I might have given it to the wrong person, or perhaps not waited long enough for the right person. I had to remind myself that I must have known to whom and when to give the book and should not think twice about it because no matter who received it, they would extract their own lesson from it.

Many years later, I came across the book at a book fair at my son's school. I quickly scooped up the few copies they had and continued to give the book when it seemed applicable to people I was meeting in my life. I am not as hung up on who may or may not be the right recipient any more. I am just grateful that I can continue to give back what someone had given to me—the priceless gift of giving and being heard and seen for who I was. The book's meaning continues to evolve and so does my gratitude.

I believe that Mrs. Parzack was an angel looking out for me. It is a tribute to her that her gift continues to give back every day. The art of giving back is easily available to all of us. We touch people in many ways every day, so why not give with the intent of giving back?

The Drive

Once I decided to publish this book and I started sharing the book with others for feedback, I was often asked: "What created the drive to take on this book? Where did it come from?" I don't think I have an exact answer; I do believe it is woven in the fabric of my life. While there are many times I have helped others, there are also countless ways I have been helped along my journey through life.

Rarely have I ever met a person who doesn't want to be heard, accepted, loved, or a part of something. This, in itself, inspires me to keep getting involved or sharing my gifts with others.

I find reaching out and being a part of something even more important given the growing world of electronics and the way it continues to become a way of life for the average person. In this world,

RARELY HAVE I MET A PERSON WHO DOESN'T WANT TO BE HEARD, ACCEPTED, OR LOVED.

we continually disengage from one another. This way of life can teach our children that separation is normal. However, there are countless events, stories, and reports that will support the fact that we are stronger when we work together. Regardless of what we want to believe, we need each other. People need people.

It is a proven fact that babies in the NICU have a higher rate of improvement when they are held and have skin-to-skin contact with another human. This passage is from the American Academy of Pediatrics on October 23, 2015, in an article called *Skin to Skin Contact with Baby in Neonatal Unit Decreases Maternal Stress Levels*:

"'We already know there are physiological benefits in the newborns when they are held skin-to-skin,' Dr. Isaza said, such as stabilization of heart rate, breathing patterns and blood oxygen levels, gains in sleep time and weight, decreased crying, greater breastfeeding success and earlier hospital discharge. 'Now we have more evidence that skin-to-skin contact can also decrease parental stress that can interfere with bonding, health and emotional wellness, and the interpersonal relations of parents, as well as breastfeeding rates.'"

This little fact is a key indicator of how we can live a better life, if we interact and empower one another.

One of the biggest lessons I learned in life was here in my community. It was the ability to receive without the ability to give. In the spring of 2012, during an oddly warm winter for Chicago, I was on the phone with a friend and decided to step outside onto the deck to take advantage of the sunny, warm, and beautiful day. As I went to lean back on the railing, without any warning, the railing gave way. I fell seven feet backwards, my head hitting the brick pavers beneath me. (I discovered later the railing was rotted away.) The emergency room staff thought I was going to be paralyzed and believed I was lucky to even be alive. I had a hematoma the size of a softball on my head, shattered bones in my right shoulder area, soft tissue damage in my spine, and contusions from head to toe on my right side. I was a mess, but my CAT scans came back without so much as a fracture in my skull (they did the scan twice to be sure) and to their surprise, I was able to walk.

I was sent home to heal. I spent the first six weeks of recovery in bed and at the doctors. My life came to a complete halt. My daughter spent the last six weeks of her senior year in high school taking care of me. When she was in school she would call and check in and made sure someone visited while she was away. My friends and community provided meals and support during those six weeks. I spent almost every day in tears, not because of my situation, but because of the outpouring of love and support. I had to learn how to receive and be grateful in a manner that is still hard to articulate.

Everyone told me that I had given so much in the past that it was my turn to receive. Did I? I wondered. In my eyes, I did not see it that way. I saw myself as only being a part of the community and thought that others did far more than I. It was truly a humbling experience, one filled with the richness of love and support from people who had been mere strangers only six years prior, when I first moved to the area.

It is safe to say that this situation could have been far different if I had kept to myself and did not get involved. The bigger lesson I learned is giving and receiving are equally important. I have found that people deeply appreciate when their help is received and it is just as empowering as giving. In the end, the ability to give and receive can create life-long friends, strengthen bonds with family and extended family, create cherished experiences and memories, and most importantly, it can build stronger communities. It supports the old saying "it takes a village." Whether that means raising your children, helping to complete a goal, or just helping out in general, it all counts.

Several months after the accident, I began experiencing short-term memory loss and the inability ability to pull common words from my memory to engage in conversation. I thought I was literally losing my mind.

I went to my doctors and after receiving weak scores for memory testing, I saw a neurologist. I was suffering from post-concussion syndrome (PCS). Apparently, after a TBI it is not uncommon to experience memory loss several months later. The neurologist gave me a list to try to follow to help me through recovery. One of the to-dos on the list was not to be alone. Apparently, you need human interaction to help keep you in a positive frame of mind, allowing you to heal better.

For me, this did not come easy. I was an empty nester, and my office was in my home. My mind was easily over-taxed and tired, making the effort seem even more daunting. I soon discovered why you do not want to be alone. When you are alone, your mind can wander and start filling you with doubt about who you are or what is happening in your life. For example: "Will I ever heal? Will people even want to work with me if I cannot remember anything? Am I this or am I..." It is a very dark voice, and I imagine, a voice unique to each person's life and experiences.

During these times, I worked at not being alone. Even a call to a friend to share what was going on or to listen to what was going on in their lives helped. Listening took my mind off me! Other people can bring us hope to continue to fight the fight and move through life until we can manage on our own.

As a trained chef, I do love when food and community come together. It is a great way to strengthen community. Start at home by teaching your children to enjoy a family meal together, unplugged from electronics and engaged in simple, everyday conversations. Even if you do this once a week it will bring family closer together.

11

A family dinner does not necessarily have to be with our immediate family. Create a space by opening your home for dinner with your friends or neighbors, especially if you live on your own. Everyone can bring a dish to share and if cooking is not their "thing," they can help in other ways. Just make sure everyone is invited to be included. When we gather together and talk about our days over a meal, it builds friendships and brings family closer.

I love the current community I am a part of. I jokingly refer to it as "Mayberry on steroids." It is a fine combination of an urban and suburban environment in Oak Park, Illinois. People are friendly. They smile and say hello to strangers and friends. I find the people I meet are active in the community and try to work together to make a positive pathway for all. I have seen parents hold their children accountable and instill the importance of being an active part in the community by example and having the kids get involved. I often compare the goodwill of others in my area to myself, to see if I am doing all that I can. I realize that not all communities are perfect, and Oak Park is no exception, but I am inspired by my friends and my experiences.

I was truly blessed to be able to finish raising my children here and calling the Chicagoland area my home. Since I have arrived, I have been fortunate to make many new friends and acquaintances. I am part of a choir, led by and filled with talented and loving people at Ascension Church. I am in a loving and embracing book club called Talking Heads, filled with empowering and strong women. I credit the kindness of others reaching out, of joining activities I embrace, and sticking with it them for making the most of opportunities presented.

CREATING A CHANGE

We can find a surplus of quotes to inspire us, from our family members to greats like Albert Einstein or Maya Angelou. Sports are not really my thing, but for the sake of looking at our efforts to drive change, I love these three quotes by Wayne Gretzky:

"You miss 100 percent of the shots you never take." This quote can help us to acknowledge that we will miss opportunities we don't take, and open the door to regret or question why we didn't do something.

"I skate to where the puck is going to be, not to where it has been." If you don't like the way your community is or what you are doing; take a shot at being an advocate for creating change. Don't spend time looking at how it got there, but where you can help take it.

"A good hockey player plays where the puck is and a great hockey player plays where the puck is going to be." We are all moving forward. Being aware of your surroundings is important, but working to bring community where it can be is priceless.

No matter how grim things may seem, that "diamond ring" of light is always shining. When we acknowledge this light and begin to turn our thoughts toward it, we will be able to change our ways. We can achieve anything if we set our hearts and minds to it, if not today then tomorrow, and if not tomorrow, the next day. The key is to appreciate what we have now and persist. The more we appreciate, the more we realize how much we already have. Recognize the gift for even its smallest essence and be grateful for it. Eventually that gratefulness will nourish every aspect of your world. Everywhere we turn today we are bombarded by marketing—mottos, slogans, buzz-words—all captivating and promising abundance. But if we keep seeking what we need outside of ourselves, we may miss what we already have—ourselves, our individuality, the largest asset we possess and control, whether we realize it or not. If we stop, take a step back, and take a good look at ourselves, we just may find the answers.

Take a pragmatic view of how you want to invest your "wealth" for the greatest return with no strings attached for the receiver of your gift. The best and the most meaningful gifts we give are unconditional, from the heart, with no expectations in return.

Begin by asking yourself a few questions: Who am I? What are my gifts and talents? If I could do one thing right now to make a difference, what would it be?

Perhaps you would like to learn more about something. You might be able to learn and help at the same time. Often when we do offer help, we learn that it broadens our world and our experiences.

Do not discount any ideas about how you can make a difference that come to mind, and if something doesn't come to you immediately, don't worry about it. Sometimes we need a little nudge; that is what this book is about. It is meant to be the spark to ignite a flame, no matter what size. Each chapter provides a starting point and a place to write or share your gifts.

The book highlights ways in which people have been giving back and will touch every reader differently. Giving back is the purest form of love when offered unconditionally and without expectations, resulting in an expanded sense of gratitude and filling an inner emptiness. Millions of people do it every day and have done it in times past. They have led us, followed others, or just decided to be a part of something greater. There is no perfect time to begin to broaden our awareness. Do it when the time is right for you.

You do not have to be Mother Teresa; you just need to be you. Can you imagine a world in which everyone joined their personal talents together to give back? Imagine a world more balanced and filled with love for our individual selves: a world of compassion and support for others. Imagine a world of love felt in our inmost heart, deeper than a spoken word. Generations will be

YOU DO NOT HAVE TO BE MOTHER TERESA; YOU JUST NEED TO BE YOU.

grateful and we will thrive. This generation and generations to follow will then build on our example of change, continuing to grow as a culture and a society by giving back. One by one, one step at a time, joining together in our own unique way—this is the change. So let's get rolling and create a snowball effect. And who wants to stand in the way of a rolling snowball?

This book starts with some ideas for lending a hand. Each section allows room for you to add ideas of your own and build the steps to achieve the goal of 100 percent participation. The intention is to be a catalyst that encourages you yourself to be the change. Write your ideas down and put them into action, or simply share the steps you are already taking to encourage others to join the efforts of bringing communities closer and making them stronger—today and for years to come.

The Road Map

I often thought having a handy guide about life attached to us when we came into this world could prove to be quite useful. Something equivalent to a road map or a guide to direct us through our daily life. We would know how to raise our children for the best possible outcome, how to interact with our family and friends, and how to exchange conversation with others that are just passing through. The list can go on. Since that is not an option, we are left to decide how to make our lives the best we can and how to make others lives we pass along on the road of life better too!

Over the years, I have developed what I call my tool box. My tool box is filled with lessons I have learned along the way and I keep handy for life's experiences. Much like a video game, we find nuggets along the way to be used to help us out when we need them.

The list below includes a few tools in my tool box to help me navigate through what I call the road map of life. Life likes to throw up roadblocks and detours. It is not the roadblocks and detours that matter, but how we respond to them.

TOOLS FROM MY TOOL BOX:
1.   The world is already perfect.

2.   We do not need to solve all the world's problems.

3. Just one little pebble in the water ripples out to places we are unable to see from our present vantage point.

4. It is not our role to judge.

5. What works for us may not work for someone else.

6. Listen.

7. Support.

8. It doesn't have to cost a dime.

9. Some help is better than no help.

10. Share your ideas with people who ask.

ACT!

These tools can help you move through the roadblocks or detours on any road map of life. You may hit a few along the way, but like driving home, even though you can't see your home, you know it is there. You know that if you encounter an accident, a traffic jam, or road construction, you either wait patiently for it to clear or you take a detour. The point is, you get home—perhaps not the way you originally planned, but you still arrive. You can see your home in your mind's eye and visualize what you need to do to get there, and you keep driving until eventually you do. It's not that different for anything else you want to achieve. That's why you make plans, and if you get sidetracked, you look at a map and figure out another way to get there.

I have elaborated further to help you understand the benefits of the nuggets in this tool box. You can refer to it as a guide if you need help along the way.

THE WORLD IS ALREADY PERFECT

Some objections spring to mind, but the world really is perfect. If it weren't, you wouldn't be here. Shift your thoughts to abundance. Be grateful for what you have. View the world as perfect and your actions will lend a hand to another person who wants to make a difference. Remember, the world is only as perfect as we choose to see it. Ask yourself, what would I do if the world were perfect? Try seeing yourself doing it; then it will be easier to create it. If you can't see it, it will be harder to accomplish. Everything originates from a thought.

WE DO NOT NEED TO SOLVE ALL THE WORLD'S PROBLEMS

Why go out and try to tackle an impossibly huge task on our own when we can focus on what we each do best and allow the hands of many to paint the larger picture? Again, many hands make light work. If you have an idea but need help bringing it to fruition, share it with others to see if they can help. Support and teamwork pave the way, even if it is only one person's vision.

JUST ONE LITTLE PEBBLE IN THE WATER RIPPLES OUT TO PLACES WE ARE UNABLE TO SEE FROM OUR PRESENT VANTAGE POINT

A stone thrown into a pond starts a ripple effect whose rings will eventually touch places in the water and the land that are not visible to you here and now. All you know is that you are a part of the change you created. The effects of a small, kind action can be far-reaching. You may never know how many people that kind action will touch or how far it will spread.

IT IS NOT OUR ROLE TO JUDGE

This is related to #3 above. We cannot determine or really know how our actions will affect someone, because we are not privy to that person's mind and thoughts. Our kind gesture may seem to go unnoticed or be a complete waste of time. But the recipient simply may not know how to express feelings of gratitude. Or our action might change the way the recipient makes a choice in the next minute or even years from now. So always choose a kind option.

WHAT WORKS FOR US MAY NOT WORK FOR SOMEONE ELSE

We are all individuals, blessed with gifts and talents unique to our lives, even if some of us have similar gifts. We create thoughts derived from many experiences perceived with our own senses. Our experiences combined with compassion can place us in the right position to help someone else in similar circumstances. At the same time, do not be offended if the other person declines to accept your help. Just be grateful you had the opportunity to offer it; let them work it through from there and assure them that you are available if needed.

LISTEN

Try to quiet the mind chatter and take time to really listen to everyone around you. If you feel that this is not a strength of yours, begin by practicing on your friends or family. Try asking some questions: What would you like to do? What do you want help with? Repeat what you heard back to them and see if they agree with what you heard, or if they were actually trying to say something different. If it is different, then you have a chance to ask some questions to gain a better understanding. When you actually practice this, you may come to understand that sometimes you do not need to do anything further; just the act of listening helps. However, if you are asked for help, it is easier to provide what they really need. If you can't provide what is asked for, you now have a better understanding in order to guide them to someone who can.

SUPPORT

Support someone's idea for making a positive impact by acknowledging what they want to do and encouraging them to do their best—with no negative comments. When someone shares an idea, many people feel compelled to offer their own knowledge or direction without being asked for it. Even though you may know more, remember to ask if they want to hear about it; then let them make their own choice. You may never know what they can accomplish using their own ideas and methods. Walt Disney is often quoted as saying, "If you can dream it, you can achieve it." Support helps a person keep up the good work, even if they get discouraged. We may never know how our support will affect someone's life. So be positive and supportive. You never know the reach of the ripple or the size of the pond.

IT DOES NOT HAVE TO COST A DIME

Just because you want to help does not mean you have to reach your hand into your pocket. It is not wise to give beyond your means. Giving back is not just about writing a check; it is about the heart to the hand, rolling up your sleeves and doing something. From offering a smile to a sad friend to one of the many suggestions in this book and beyond, in the end, every little bit helps.

SOME HELP IS BETTER THAN NO HELP
Even the smallest act contributes to making a difference. The important thing is that you reach out and help, knowing that one person can make even a little difference.

SHARE YOUR IDEAS WITH PEOPLE WHO ASK
When someone asks, provide what help you can give. When someone requests help, they love getting it. If someone notices the work you have been doing, for example, they may ask you for advice about how they can try to achieve similar goals.

ACT!

This may appear to be a logical next step, but how often can you think of things to do but never act on your best intentions? The reasons for not acting are many, but in the end most of them are excuses, especially if you are thinking of something well within your means.

Even the most generous thought of loving actions does not end up loving anyone when not put into action. Act on your positive intentions.

This book is a great example. When the idea came to me, it was easy to dismiss it, not start, or procrastinate, but unless I continued to follow it through, the book would never have landed in your hands and you would not be reading it.

HELPFUL HINTS
Keep these in mind as you read about the different ways you can make a difference in a community.

A few things are important to remember when offering your services to existing organizations.

1. CALL first. Learn about special needs the organizations may have. You may find they are not a good fit for you, or perhaps you can offer something completely different than you'd anticipated.

2. SHARE your talents and skills and ask how they can be helpful to that particular group or person.

3. SPREAD THE WORD. If you are aware that an organization needs the skills of a particular kind of person, take the opportunity to talk about it among friends and family or in social settings. If you hear of a need that matches someone else's skills, you can pass the word along.

4. If you COMMIT, follow through.

5. Do not bite off more than you can chew. BE REALISTIC about your time and abilities.

6. COMMUNICATE while you are working on a project. Then, if something takes longer than anticipated or you cannot complete the project, the organization will be better able to help get the job done.

7. If a VOLUNTEER opportunity does not work well for you, do not stop reaching out. Continue to look until you find something that works best for you and the community.

8. If you are not comfortable speaking directly to an organization initially, go to the INTERNET to learn more about what you would like to do.

9. Be open to TRANSFORMATION. Very seldom is there a one-way exchange. Try looking at it as something you will do with, not for, others. You may learn something new about yourself or the place/person you are helping and this may be something of great value to you. It comes down to being changed by the experience in a way you were not expecting when you started.

MAKING THE MOST OF THIS BOOK

The next section describes several different communities. Each one offers ideas for action, tells a short story, and provides space to write down a new idea or to note something you have already done in that community. It is meant to get the ball rolling and inspire one another with the encouragement necessary to strengthen our communities every day. I want to hear from you, so let your supportive voice be heard.

This is a starting point to join together to empower ourselves and others. Together we can grow these efforts and expand beyond the stories and communities found in this book. Here's how to start:

PAY IT FORWARD

- Share this book with someone. Help keep the good intentions of my first grade teacher's work alive.

- If you feel so inclined, go to HeartToHandsMovement. com to sponsor a classroom to share in the Heart To Hands Tree project.

WRITE DOWN YOUR IDEAS

- If an idea is sparked while reading about ways you can help in one of the many communities listed in the book, add it to the Idea Incubator area of that section. Writing an idea down helps you remember and it may be more likely you will act on it.

- Put it into action.

SHARE YOUR STORIES

- Write down your own stories that come to mind while you are reading in the Share Pot area. Share them on our Facebook Heart To Hands Movement community page, and use one of our frames to post a picture showing what you are doing to help make a difference and what is possible.

TALK ABOUT IT WITH FRIENDS

- Build a community group.
- Meet once a month to learn more and share.

HOLD A COMMUNITY EVENT

- See if your town can invite local organizations to offer information sessions about ways people can help in your community.
- Volunteer to help promote the event.

Check with organizations to learn what they are seeking in terms of help, or how your own ideas can make a difference.

CHILDREN'S HOSPITALS

**TIME CAN BE THE BEST GIFT.
TOO MANY CHILDREN
NEVER HAVE A VISITOR.**

1. Read to the children. Pick up some favorite funny children's books and devote time being a reader.

2. Visit the children who seldom or never see a visitor grace their bedside, and have a good laugh with each other.

3. Hold a craft day. Find activities that keep children engaged and pay close attention to their every need.

4. Play a game; a new one or an old favorite.

5. Tutor.

6. Create a mini scavenger hunt for children who can participate.

Children's hospitals have a very special place in my heart. My brother spent most of his infancy and toddlerhood in and out of surgeries. We spent a lot of time in the hospital as a family, and I saw what a special place it was. But at the same time, I saw how many children spent too many hours alone. My biggest eye opener came when I stepped off the elevator on the wrong floor one day and realized that I was on the burn floor. A playpen holding three toddlers happily playing with one another was set in front of the nurses' station. All three were severely burned and had lost part of an arm or leg, had severe scarring on various parts of their bodies or other bodily damage as a result of their burns. I was awestruck. Being a child, I innocently asked why they were not in their rooms. The kindly nurse replied that they were all alone and never had visitors; playing with the other patients helped them laugh.

When I was in college, I had an opportunity to work with my school to create a gingerbread town for a charity event for the local children's hospital. I had fun, but I decided to shift my efforts to decorating gingerbread people with the children. I remembered how important interaction with these children is. I asked Children's Hospital of Detroit if we could have a gingerbread decorating day and pass out decorated cookies to the patients who could not participate. The hospital welcomed the idea and we set a day, with clear instructions that the decorated cookies be presented as ornaments because of various dietary restrictions.

My children and I hosted a gingerbread cookie decorating party at our home to make enough cookies for all the patients, leaving several to be decorated with the children who could join us in the craft room. The age requirement to volunteer was sixteen. My children were under sixteen at the time, so a few friends and I went to the hospital to distribute and decorate cookies with the young patients.

It was a huge success, filled with smiles and laughter. We continued our cookie decorating day for several more years. My father was a member of the Kiwanis Club of Garden City, Michigan and shared what we were doing. Since Children's Hospital is one of the approved groups that Kiwanis helps, they pitched in, volunteered, and paid for all the ingredients, eliminating my out-of-pocket expenses. Since volunteering is an everyday opportunity, we decided to expand our efforts to Valentine's Day and substituted hearts for the gingerbread— a great way to spread the love. Please call the volunteer office to share your ideas and learn more about the opportunities available for volunteers and the requirements needed to ensure a positive experience is had by all.

IDEA INCUBATOR

_____

_____

_____

_____

_____

SHARE POT

_____

_____

_____

_____

_____

Homeless Shelters

**NOT EVERYONE NEEDS CLOTHES.
THE LIST IS LONG. YOU MIGHT BE SURPRISED
AT HOW YOUR TIME AND HOSPITALITY CAN
CHANGE YOUR ENTIRE PERSPECTIVE.**

We can easily walk past a person lying in the street or on a park bench, or pass judgment without understanding their real circumstances.

1. Volunteer at a local shelter or soup kitchen and help serve meals. (Please remember to call a local shelter to start to learn more about ways you can contribute to making a difference in the homeless community.)

2. Cook extra for dinner and bring it to someone on the street.

3. Engage in conversations. Say hello. Acknowledge a person's humanity.

4. Assist with repair projects in a shelter.

5. Create a donation drive at your school or church for items needed at the local shelter. Make it a party.

6. Save your toiletries from hotels when you travel and oral hygiene giveaways from the dentist. Donate them to a shelter or center that assists the homeless.

When my daughter and a friend were in eighth grade they began a manicure ministry with the help of the friend's mother through Old St. Patrick's Parish in Chicago. Every month for the next five years, the girls, the other mother, and I went to a homeless shelter in Chicago and gave manicures, hand massages, snacks, goodie bags provided by Old St. Pat's, and warm conversation. Several people donated the nail polish and other items we needed to get started. This effort was slow at first, but as the women at the shelter began to feel more comfortable we enjoyed many conversations and laughs. There's nothing like a little TLC to make a person's spirit shine.

One of our sessions fell during Hurricane Katrina. I was working with a group of people who were creating meal kits for FEMA to distribute and my phone was ringing constantly during our time at the shelter with calls from that group. One of residents asked why I was getting so many calls. When I explained, the shelter resident, homeless herself for the first time, asked, "How can I help? I would like to volunteer my time to help pack food." Here was a prime example that no matter what life hands us, we can all make a difference. I was extremely touched by such a beautiful gift of compassion. Before my daughter and her friend left for college, the women living at the shelter asked the director if they could have a going-away party for them. The director happily helped the woman give the girls a little party and a meaningful gift to express their gratitude. It was overwhelmingly beautiful.

Homelessness can touch any one of us for one reason or another. Try putting yourself in a homeless person's shoes and ask yourself what you would enjoy. Then ask yourself, "What can I do?"

IDEA INCUBATOR

SHARE POT

RETIREMENT CENTERS AND NURSING HOMES

HAVE YOU EVER THOUGHT
THAT SENIORS MIGHT HAVE A LOT
TO OFFER YOU?

1. Adopt a grandparent. Bring your family and children to engage in activities.

2. Open your business or place of work for a tour or activity for a local center.

3. Share your talent (playing the piano, singing, the arts, etc.)

4. Help design and plant flower and vegetable gardens.

5. Type emails or write letters for residents.

6. Bring your pet to visit with residents.

A professional Broadway dancer with Alzheimer's disease in an assisted living center had good and bad days, but she held her memories of dancing dear to her heart. Whenever she engaged in sharing memories of her dancing days she lit up with joy. It so happened that a friend of a worker at the center was directing *The Nutcracker* with a local dance company. Remembering her resident's passion, she asked the local company if they would give her a couple of tickets so the resident could attend the ballet, if the family agreed. Not only did the company perform for the resident, they gave her and her family a private performance for their final dress rehearsal. The night was filled with love and joy, and as she sat there watching the dress rehearsal, she too participated by engaging her feet in the steps. According to her family, the resident said that this was the kindest, most loving, and most thoughtful thing anyone had ever done for her. When you reach out to a retirement center or nursing home, they will be more than happy to assist you to make the most of your volunteer time!

IDEA INCUBATOR

_____

_____

_____

_____

_____

SHARE POT

_____

_____

_____

_____

_____

MAGIC HAPPENS WHEN PRESCHOOLS ARE IN
NURSING HOMES. IN THE 1970s, JAPAN STARTED
TO PUT PRESCHOOLS IN NURSING HOMES.
SLOWLY THE IDEA SPREAD WORLD WIDE.
THERE ARE NOW A NUMBER OF FACILITIES
THAT HOST A PRESCHOOL, IN TURN BRINGING
MEASURABLE POSITIVE IMPACTS FOR BOTH THE
CHILDREN AND ITS RESIDENTS.

Poverty

ANY COMMUNITY MIGHT CONTAIN INDIVIDUALS OR FAMILIES LIVING IN POVERTY. POVERTY IS WOVEN INTO EVERY COMMUNITY.

1. Pick up some extra groceries when you go shopping and drop them off at a food bank.

2. Encourage your teens to join a club or organization that focuses on giving back to the community. It will keep them involved and help them learn to appreciate the abundance in their own lives.

3. Join a group like the Appalachia Service Project (ASP) or Habitat for Humanity and help repair existing homes or build new ones.

4. Volunteer at a local food bank.

5. Donate blankets, flashlights, and other eme gency items to local service organizations to offer clients so they can to be prepared in times of storms or other disasters.

6. Find out if a family in your local parish or congregation can use your talents to help with résumé writing, cooking a meal, babysitting, driving, etc.

A person or family is living in poverty when the household's gross income is less than what is necessary to maintain a healthy baseline living environment. Poverty can live right next door, and not only in areas known for lower incomes.

My son and a group of other teens went with an organization called Young Neighbors in Action (YNIA) to Tijuana, Mexico, where they worked on various projects throughout the community. He noted upon his return that he had never been exposed to such poverty. But most amazing to him was the amount of joy and happiness people living in the community shared while helping one another in all circumstances.

My daughter went to the Appalachian Mountains with other teens with the Appalachia Service Project (ASP). In the poorest county in America they worked directly with families to repair and build structures in and around the homes, creating better living conditions. She learned how to install insulation, put up drywall, tape, spackle, and paint. She repaired holes in walls and played with animals infested with fleas. She left knowing that she would return every summer, and so she did during high school.

You need not go to another country or even another state; these stories were pulled from opportunities the teens chose to be involved in. The next year my son's YNIA group went to work in Detroit. Their work area was located half a mile from the school he attended before we moved to the Chicagoland area. Poverty stands at the threshold of many doors in America. Even if you do not actually live next door, you can aid people who are working and living in poverty in several ways.

If you choose to work through an organization to help with poverty, take the time to learn a little more about the many opportunities they have available or pick up the phone and share some ideas you have and see if it is a good fit!

IDEA INCUBATOR

_____

_____

_____

_____

_____

_____

SHARE POT

_____

_____

_____

_____

_____

_____

General Hospitals

WHERE ARE ALL
THE CANDY STRIPERS?

Although you do not see candy stripers in many hospitals nowadays, there is still a great need for volunteers to keep the heart of the hospital strong and vibrant. You can go to a hospital's website or go its volunteer services office to learn about service opportunities.

1. Bedside visiting can be as vital to well-being as a doctor's prescription.

2. Start a "Just Because" box at home, your place of work, or at your school. Fill it with uplifting cards or crafts and bring it to the local hospital to distribute.

3. Do office or clerical work.

4. Knit blankets, hats, or shawls for patients.

5. Be a greeter.

6. Play cards or board games with patients.

Community is a high priority at the University of Chicago Medical Center. It may not be in the news, but every day families and patients feel the support. When a father passed away after a long illness, his family was very grateful for the love and care he and they received during the time they spent there. Ever since, for more than twelve years now, the entire family visits every patient at Christmastime, with one person dressed as Santa Claus delivering a candy cane and a cuddly bear in a bag. They realized how valuable the time and sharing was to a patient. Christmas for adults in a hospital can be just as hard as in the children's ward, if not harder. The family has made a commitment to continue this tradition not only in their generation but for their future generations. They realize that donating visiting time can be more valuable than just donating funds.

Please remember to pick up the phone and speak to the volunteer department when planning on volunteering at your local hospital. They will help make your experience a fulfilling one. And don't be shy to share ideas you have, because your unique idea may be something they have not done and will be welcomed. Making sure it fits into their guidelines will be helpful!

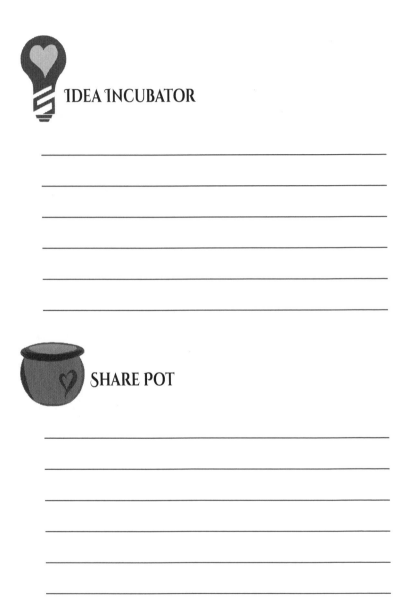

IDEA INCUBATOR

_____

_____

_____

_____

_____

_____

SHARE POT

_____

_____

_____

_____

_____

_____

THE GREATEST GIFT YOU CAN SHARE WITH
ANOTHER IS KINDNESS, LOVE AND APPRECIATION.
SHARING YOUR GOODNESS AT A HOSPITAL
IS THE CANDY STRIPER OF TODAY!

VA Hospitals

MEDICAL CARE AND COMMUNITY
ALL IN ONE.

Every Veteran's Administration hospital is unique in its own way. I was told at one VA hospital that if you've met one, you've met one. Start by learning what your local VA hospital needs most. There are countless opportunities here with several branches that reach out even further.

1. Offer your time to guide and direct patients.

2. Provide gently used clothing for veterans in need.

3. Put together care packages to bring to the VA hospital for distribution to our homeless veterans and the patients in the hospital (toiletries, combs, creams, deodorant, toothbrushes, toothpaste). These items are needed here just as much as overseas.

4. Bring toys to donate throughout the year so ill veterans can give a gift to their children for a birthday or holiday.

5. Volunteer to help with clerical duties.

6. Spend one-on-one time with a veteran, reading or playing a game.

These soldiers have the ultimate gift to others—their service. Whether or not you agree with the war in which they served, these troops should be recognized for their efforts. It is not possible to imagine what that experience was like unless you have marched in their boots, but it is possible to give compassion, support, and acceptance.

VA hospitals are a government entity, so their operations depend on the budget allocated by the government. The hospitals can only accept any type of donation through the office for volunteer services. So whether you are volunteering time, donating money, supplying a need, or offering other services as needed, your help is greatly appreciated. Contact your VA volunteer office to learn more.

Involvement with a VA hospital makes a strong impact. Many of the volunteers are veterans themselves. Some are even homeless or on the verge of homelessness. This opportunity to give back provides a sense of belonging to a group. In many cases, the veteran volunteers have had their lives turned around by this simple act of kindness.

One veteran volunteered his time to complete forty hours of community service. A thousand-plus hours later he is still actively volunteering. This man has been through a lot and does not know where he would be without the volunteering service. When he gets up every morning, it is still hard sometimes to do the right thing, but he knows that if he is not there by nine o'clock, the volunteer office will miss him and will know that something is wrong. Without the volunteer service, he knows that no one would know or even care where he was at nine o'clock in the morning. It has helped him realize that he is important to some people, whereas before he did not think he was important to anyone.

Many stories are unfolding every day in all kinds of communities. Try to learn some of them. You will not regret it.

IDEA INCUBATOR

SHARE POT

NEIGHBORS

INTRODUCE YOURSELF.
THE OPPORTUNITY TO GIVE BACK
CAN BE AS CLOSE AS NEXT DOOR.

1. If you like to bake, share a dozen cookies with a neighbor.

2. Work on organizing a block party. Get others involved and provide a fun venue for neighbors to get to know each other.

3. A small picnic or meal for a few of your neighbors can provide a gateway for getting to know them.

4. Check in on an elderly neighbor and see if you can pick up some groceries when you head to the store.

5. Offer to help a family with a sick or injured member who may be struggling. Bring over a meal or help with housework or driving.

6. Make a daily effort to say hello and ask your neighbors how they're doing.

How well do you know your neighbors? Most of these suggestions work better if you take the time to get to know who lives next door to you. There is no one perfect place to start, but rest assured that taking the time to get to know your neighbors can have serious side effects, including but not limited to new friendships, support, comfort, and perhaps the occasional laugh. Plus, getting to know your neighbors will always yield opportunities to help and give back.

In August of 2003, we lost our electricity during the great power outage that lasted for days in parts of Ohio, New York, Michigan, and Canada. Our area in Michigan was without power for four days. It so happened that we had on hand a bouncy slide from a birthday party, along with the generator that was required for its operation—a blessing in disguise. We now had a generator to see us through; the only thing we needed was gas. First, the children went around to the neighbors and asked if they needed anything from the store. Then, with only a quarter of a tank of gas in my car and an empty gas can to fill, we headed out. We did not find an area with power for over fifty miles, and had to wait in a very long line in hopes of obtaining some gas. The kids ran in to the store and got a few of the odds and ends requested, we were able to get gas, and headed home.

For the next few days, our kitchen was a gathering place for morning coffee and meals. The neighbors were all outdoors and got to know each other. I heard about more positive experiences from this little "hiccup" in modern life than negative. Even in Manhattan, people calmly and collectedly walked home over the bridges and streets, while incidents of looting were reported to be few and far between, making national news. For the first time, people stepped outside and interacted with their neighbors, had some fun, and learned a lot about each other. Sometimes we get so caught up in our own little world with all its modern-day conveniences that we lose touch with the people right under our noses.

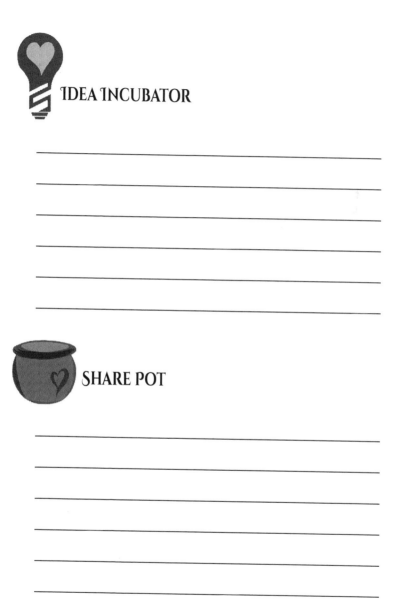

IDEA INCUBATOR

_____

_____

_____

_____

_____

SHARE POT

_____

_____

_____

_____

_____

_____

SCHOOLS

**YOU CAN HELP EVEN IF YOU DO
NOT HAVE A CHILD IN SCHOOL.**

While schools are designed to foster growth and offer positive support, they are also great places to share your talents and set an example of giving back. As with many organizations, schools can vary dramatically within the same community. Even with so many budget cuts, schools offer many ways to help enhance the life experiences of our youth in order to create a stronger community tomorrow. Remember to contact your local school first to see what you can offer.

1. Organize and stuff folders and files.

2. Assist with art projects.

3. Tutor children who are struggling academically.

4. Donate classroom materials. Host a party and ask everyone to bring a needed item.

5. Donate outdoor activity items, such as jump ropes, balls, or games.

6. Organize support for families with sick children or adults. Offer help with meals or carpooling.

Dana, a full-time working mother, spends time giving back to the community by volunteering at her daughter's school. It brings her great joy to have this extra time to be involved in her daughter's life and to volunteer at the school. One day, while waiting to pick up her daughter, she met a single mother with a child at the school and an infant at home. They quickly became friends. This mother was not able to enjoy the same opportunities to volunteer at her daughter's school because she did not have someone to care for the infant if she wanted to spend this time with her daughter. Dana understood what this school time meant to her and wanted to help, so she volunteered to babysit and give the other woman an opportunity to have the same experience. Their friendship has continued, and they now swap babysitting for each other's children when needed.

IDEA INCUBATOR

_____

_____

_____

_____

_____

_____

SHARE POT

_____

_____

_____

_____

_____

_____

We never know where inspiration can stem from. When I shared the drawing of the tree for the book cover with my friend David, he called and suggested that the tree could be a great activity for classes or a family project. I shared the idea with some teachers to get their input and they loved it. The Heart to Hands Tree Project was born. The project engages children to learn about ways to think outside of their world and take small doable steps to make a difference in others lives. The activity involves a poster with a bare tree. When a student does a kind act towards others, they are given a "seeded heart leaf" by their teacher and they place it on the tree. When the tree is full, the students collectively plant the heart leaves to beautify an area with flowers.

Learn how you can pay it forward with this project. Go to:
HeartToHandsMovement.com/HeartToHandsTreeProject

1. Pick the project(s) package that you want to share.

2. Choose a classroom you want to sponsor or we will assign one to you.

3. We mail the project to the classroom.

4. The teacher discusses the book with the students.

5. When the student shares a kind action towards another person, they place a heart leaf on the tree.

6. The students share the completed tree and plant the seeded paper in an area to beautify the community.

7. Classes can share their work on-line and a thank you note to the donor, encouraging others to do the same.

Children working together and being kind to others are building steps to a stronger community.

Sponsor a classroom. Build a Future. A portion of the proceeds helps support teachers to get the tools they need to teach in their classroom.

Animals

ANIMALS PLAY A LARGE ROLE IN OUR COMMUNITIES AND CAN TOUCH AND BE TOUCHED BY PEOPLE'S LOVING ACTIONS.

Animals play a large role in many people's lives and are an important source of love and affection. Many people believe that animal shelters have plenty of help, but in truth there is an ongoing need.

1. Be a dog walker at a shelter or an animal care league.

2. Share your loving pet with sick or lonely people in the neighborhood, hospitals, or retirement centers.

3. Write to your elected official or community leaders on related animal issues.

4. Volunteer at animal hospitals or shelters.

5. Share a bag of pet food with a struggling family that has animals.

6. Set up a bird sanctuary or fish tank at a hospice center.

Abused animals are not news, but they can be the most loving pets. You may believe that you are the caretaker in your relationship with your pet, but I have found that a pet also can look after you and fulfill your nurturing needs. A pet provides unconditional love and compassion and is a great listener. Furthermore, taking a dog for a walk is beneficial to your own health by keeping you active. If you are thinking about getting an animal, check out your local kennel first and meet the animals in search of a home. You just may be surprised.

We adopted a Shar Pei from a rescue society. He had been severely abused by his previous owner, but this did not cause King to become mean himself. He was strong as an ox and let the children embrace him and play with him endlessly. He became a part of our family instantly and brought great joy with him. His story is a reminder that every life is precious.

For all you animal lovers, call your local shelter or rescue group and see how you can make a difference to help them run and take care of loving pets that have been left behind.

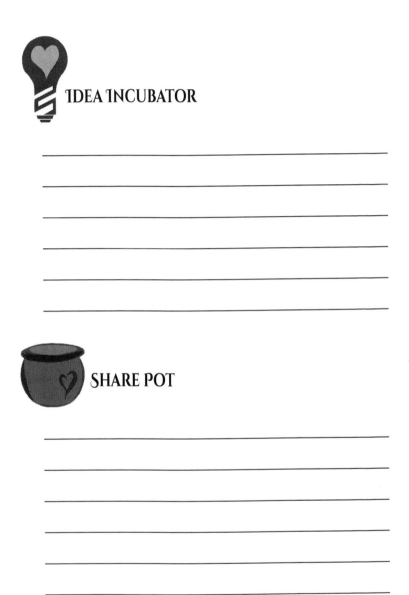

IDEA INCUBATOR

_____
_____
_____
_____
_____
_____

SHARE POT

_____
_____
_____
_____
_____
_____

ANIMALS ARE AN INSTRUMENT
OF UNCONDITIONAL LOVE.
SHARE YOUR LOVE AND LOVE WILL BE
RETURNED IN COUNTLESS WAYS.

Beautification

**YOU MIGHT BE SURPRISED AT WHAT A
LITTLE CLEAN-UP OR GARDENING CAN DO
TO LIFT THE SPIRITS OF A COMMUNITY.**

1. Clean up a run-down vacant house.

2. Plant flowers in a park.

3. Use leftover paint to refresh worn-out markings
    in play areas.

4. Help with local clean-up efforts.

5. Clean up roadsides.

6. Assist a neighbor who may need help with yard
    work or minor outside house repairs.

Help can be as simple as raking leaves. Every year my son's Boy Scout troop raked the leaves of an elderly man called Woody. He himself had been a Scout when Scouting first came to America. He lived on a large lot with lots of trees, and when the raking became too much for him it provided an opportunity for the boys to help and give back to a fellow Scout. The kids loved to listen to his stories and telling them became a highlight for him. Watching the Scouting tradition continue to run strong meant a great deal to Woody, so the boys decided to make him an honorary member of their troop. They continued to help him for several years, until his passing. Some Boy Scouts set out to rake leaves for an elderly man—and he made an everlasting impression on them.

You do not need to know someone who needs help raking their leaves. It is easy to call your local city ordinance office to learn the easiest way to accomplish your goal or learn more about other opportunities that can help beautify your town's living environment.

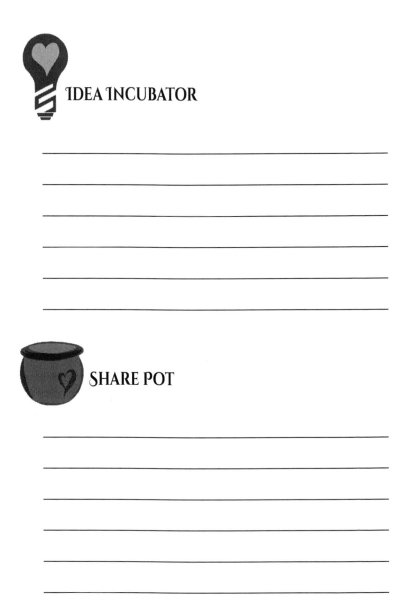

IDEA INCUBATOR

SHARE POT

FLOWERS ARE MOTHER NATURE'S
KALEIDOSCOPES OF COLOR.
THEY ARE CONSTANTLY CHANGING
AND DELIGHTING US IN AN ARRAY OF VARIETY.
SHARE SOME TODAY!

YOURSELF

LOVING YOURSELF AND HAVING FUN CAN ITSELF BRING POSITIVE CHANGE IN THE WORLD AROUND YOU. THE BEST PART IS THAT THIS ONLY REQUIRES YOUR OWN PERMISSION!

1. Try to learn something new every day. Share what you learn.

2. Take care of your body by being active and feeding yourself foods that give you proper energy and do not deplete your health.

3. Take time out every day to quiet your mind. Start small and build up to longer periods. Enjoy just being still.

4. Use kind words when talking with others, even in times of disagreement.

5. Pick up a book about something you would like to strengthen in yourself. Put your reading into practice.

6. Find something to laugh about as often as possible. Set a goal to laugh once a day.

You are one of the most significant parts of the community. Think about your actions. Kindness and compassion spread just as easily as anger and bitterness. Choosing to move in the world with mindfulness can lift not just your own spirit, but also that of others you encounter.

Easy to say, perhaps, and you may even wonder how mindfulness can be giving back to the world, but it is one of the biggest gifts you can give.

Learn to love yourself from the inside out. You are your own best friend or worst enemy. Which one do you want to be? Clearly the friend brings more joy, and the more joy you have the more joy will spill out. Happiness is just as contagious as bitterness, but happiness yields the greatest return. Begin to love yourself by setting goals that involve positive and compassionate responses, ones that are easily accomplished every day and involve your family and friends.

Know that your fear of reaching a goal is an illusion created by your own imagination. Every step you take will bring you one step closer. Feel free to share the steps you want to take, then check in and continue to share as you take them. Remember, every step brings you closer to the goals you set, so others can see and follow your direction.

IDEA INCUBATOR

_____

_____

_____

_____

_____

SHARE POT

_____

_____

_____

_____

_____

LOVE IS TRUE.
TRUE LOVE FOR YOURSELF AND FOR OTHERS IS
A BRIGHT LIGHT THAT ACTS AS A LIGHTHOUSE
TO HELP SAFELY GUIDE AND EMPOWER OTHERS.

Women's Shelters

WOMEN THERE ARE STARTING OVER. WHAT IN YOUR HOUSE CAN YOU PURGE TO GET A NEW HOME STARTED?

1. Volunteer to babysit while mothers are attending classes designed to enable them to live independently and freely.

2. Use your professional expertise to teach valuable life skills to empower these women so they can pass them down to their children.

3. Offer a "pamper night." Get a few friends together and give them a night of manicures and facials.

4. Provide diapers, formula, or a safe crib you are no longer using.

5. If you know of job opportunities, let the shelter know. A job will help the women get back on their feet with a stronger foundation to support themselves and their children.

6. Donate household items and linens to help set up a new home.

These shelters provide a safe haven for women who are homeless, have been abused, and are in need of guidance to get back on their feet. They can provide classes to learn new work skills, coping tools, and many other support systems to strengthen a woman's ability to function well on her own or with her children. Battered women are likely to re-enter abusive relationships if they cannot make changes in their lives that empower them and protect them from repeating behaviors. Even more tragic for a woman re-entering an abusive environment is the example being passed on to her children. While battered women's shelters are kept deliberately inconspicuous to protect them from abusive partners, they are in constant need of help. You can check with your local police force to learn how you can help. There are strict guidelines for most of these shelters, so take some time to learn about them in order to be able to do the most good.

Many years ago, a friend's sister was in an abusive relationship. She managed to leave, but to get started she had to leave her children and home. She was able to find a place to live and a job, but starting from scratch was a challenge. Her sister put a call out to family and friends for help. Everyone did what they could. I went through my house and was able to provide her with utensils, pots, dishes, towels, and linens. Others helped her to get back on her feet. Eventually, she was able to have her children move in with her.

That help was a game changer. Her ex-husband was confident that she would fail and come running back to the abusive marriage. She did not. Without the support of the community, she might have.

IDEA INCUBATOR

_____

_____

_____

_____

_____

SHARE POT

_____

_____

_____

_____

_____

_____

CHURCHES, CONGREGATIONS, AND OTHER HOUSES OF WORSHIP

A CHURCH CAN BE DEEPLY ROOTED IN THE COMMUNITY AND WELL-AWARE OF THE COMMUNITY'S NEEDS.

1. Bring meals or food to a shut-in member.

2. Donate gently used shoes so a child can go to school.

3. Teach in an adult literacy program.

4. Join a mentoring program for children who have fallen behind academically.

5. Adopt or mentor a senior.

6. Sort donations at the food depository.

The unspoken but understood rule requires that we avoid talking religion or politics in social settings. But we are much more than our religion or our politics. Learning to live and work with people of many different points of view is essential for strong families and communities. Worshiping congregations can provide special insight and support for the community. They are some of the best places to learn about what is needed in our community and ideal places to begin giving back to it. Making a call is the first step.

Old St. Pat's in Chicago is a stellar example of a parish with strong community programs. Not so long ago the congregation was facing a dwindling membership, but thanks to the foresight of a brilliant pastor who focused on the community, the tables have turned. The parish now has more than twenty programs that provide opportunities to make a difference in the city of Chicago. Events held throughout the year mix fun with fund-raising to finance these great causes.

Old Saint Pat's decided to rehab Su Casa, a Hispanic homeless shelter located on the South Side whose clientele is mainly women and children, most of whom are victims of domestic abuse. The building was completely run down, everything leaked, nothing was up to code, and the living conditions were dismal. The plan was to do a complete rehab, inside and out, in one day. More than 330 people signed up, so many that additional volunteers had to be redirected to other projects. The entire structure and outside environment were transformed on every level, including rehabbing a garden a quarter of a city block in size. Volunteers were so transformed by the results that today many continue to take on additional projects as need arises.

IDEA INCUBATOR

_____
_____
_____
_____
_____
_____

SHARE POT

_____
_____
_____
_____
_____
_____

WHEN WE UNITE TO EMPOWER ONE ANOTHER,
STRONGER COMMUNITIES WILL EMERGE.

TEEN CENTERS

**TEENS ARE OUR TOMORROW.
EMPOWER THEM AND THEY IN
TURN WILL EMPOWER OTHERS.**

1. Donate formal gowns, dresses and suits in good condition for first-time job interviews and high school formals.

2. Work a suicide crisis hotline. **(Please note; this much needed effort generally requires a short training session. A small investment to save the lives of those who need it.)

3. Teach life skills to the young adults.

4. Mentor youth living in high-risk environments.

5. Mentor teen mothers and fathers to teach parenting skills.

6. Share a hobby that enriches a teen and fosters fun participation or an event activity.

Centers are designed to give teens a safe and comfortable environment fostering self-empowerment, social interaction, accountability, educational support, and respect for oneself and others. They can encourage involvement in community and family and can be a place to learn new activities. There, teens can find wise and competent adults to talk to when they are having issues. Like any organization, teen centers offer a variety of different programs and activities. Contact a teen center near you to learn more and see what you can do. The center will be clear about what they need and guidelines that must be followed.

At the Corner Health Center in Ypsilanti, Michigan, there are people working to empower teens starting from age twelve through age twenty-five. Many people reach out to make a difference. The local farmer's market decided to donate tokens for the center to hand out to their teens. The tokens act as money at the farmer's market and were intended to provide the teens and young adults an opportunity to have fresh food easily available, every week. It turned out that the group had given a specific color of a token to be used. At the end of the season, the organizer came to the center to let them know that not one token had been used. The center talked with the teens and they learned that the teens did not understand what some of the produce was or how to use it, not to mention that they felt out of place at the farmer's market. A woman called to volunteer and learn ways in which she could help. They asked her if she would be willing to take a group of teens/ young adults to the farmer's market and help them to get more comfortable with the farmer's market and learn more about the produce available. In addition, the farmer's market held demonstrations at the market to teach different ways the produce could be used.

The volunteer loved what she was doing and continued to give two hours of her time each week to this project. When it began, only a few young adults participated, but as the weeks moved on, it continued to grow. After a year of giving her time, it was time to pass this program on. By this time the program was strong and many people participated. The center applied for a grant to hire someone to run it and added in cooking classes to help teach the young adults to cook on a regular basis. This all started because one person was willing to help a group of teens feel more comfortable in a new environment.

IDEA INCUBATOR

SHARE POT

THE INTERNET

KEEP THE NEWS EMPOWERING.

1. Blog to build awareness.

2. Learn more about a cause you would like to help.

3. Do some research on the many ways you can give back in a community.

4. Connect with groups and organizations that do.

5. Go social. Create a fun video about a cause you want to help and post it on social media.

6. Click it! Here are a few websites that will give back with a click.

care2.com | thehungersite.com | thenonprofits.com

We have an ongoing love/hate relationship with the world of social media, the internet, gaming, and electronics for entertainment in general. But the internet does offer easy access to information once difficult to acquire.

The internet provides a wealth of information and opportunities to help one another and our communities, locally and globally. Every effort to build awareness and strengthen our communities helps, but it is up to the individual user to decide how best to utilize this very strong and powerful tool to create change and get a project accomplished.

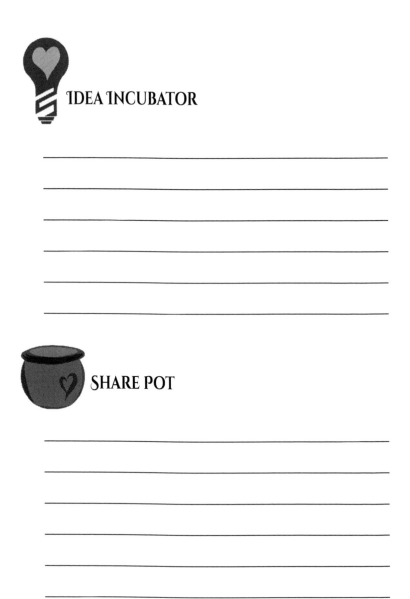

IDEA INCUBATOR

_____

_____

_____

_____

_____

_____

SHARE POT

_____

_____

_____

_____

_____

_____

_____

A GREAT WAY TO USE SOCIAL MEDIA IS TO SHOW HOW YOU AND YOUR FRIENDS ARE STRENGTHENING COMMUNITY.

- UPLOAD AND SHARE YOUR PHOTO ON THE HEART TO HANDS MOVEMENT FB PAGE.

- PLEASE FEEL FREE TO USE ONE OF OUR FRAMES (AVAILABLE UNDER HEART TO HANDS MOVEMENT IN THE FRAME SECTION OF YOUR FACEBOOK PROFILE) THAT REPRESENTS THE WORK YOU ARE DOING.

- ADD #HEARTTOHANDS TO YOUR POSTS.

Within the Country

MANY COMMUNITIES MAKE UP A COUNTRY.

1. Buy locally. Purchase goods grown or made in your area or country.

2. Purchase the products you use that support a cause; buy what you like while helping others.

3. Learn about organizations that help impoverished areas in your country and see what type of needs they have. Take action and build awareness. Invite a few friends and neighbors over and share your research with them.

4. Plan a family vacation that involves giving back to an area you have never visited and work with the community. There are several organizations in every country, such as Habitat for Humanity, Catholic Charities USA/Catholic Services, Peace Corps, Senior Corps, or Appalachia Service Project.

5. Contact your local government, let them know you would like to volunteer in communities that need extra help, and ask them to point you in the right direction.

Helping your local community is considered grassroots. When we contribute to the community we live in, it not only helps strengthen our roots where we live, it also helps lay a strong foundation to build on. From there we can reach out even further to the larger community we live in; our country. Grassroots action alone, when performed with others in every community, would make a huge difference in this country.

In every country there are areas that are not as fortunate as the community you might live in. Try to help by using the different tools offered in this book. Take it to another level by contributing to other communities across the country that need strengthening. By leading by example, we can continue positive growth, in turn strengthening our country as a whole.

The youth group at our church participates in the Appalachia Service Project. Many parishioners, in addition to the teens and adult mentors, help raise the funds to participate. They spend a week rebuilding and repairing homes to create safer living conditions for people who are not able to do so themselves. Not only does their work touch the people being helped, it transforms everyone doing the work in ways they never imagined. On our worksite one year, a child about seven years old ran up to one of the teen volunteers and embraced him. Looking at him with innocent eyes she said, "God has sent you as our angels. I know everything will be all right for us. Thank you and I love you." This experience not only affirmed the teen's efforts, it transformed the way he looked at others and confirmed that he could make a difference.

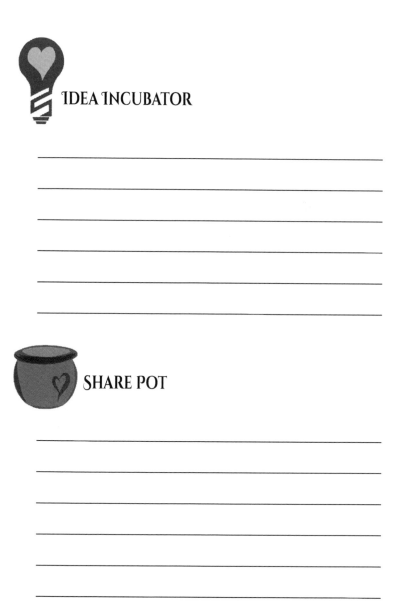

IDEA INCUBATOR

_____

_____

_____

_____

_____

_____

SHARE POT

_____

_____

_____

_____

_____

_____

Orphanages/Community Centers

THESE COMMUNITIES ARE NOT FOUND EVERYWHERE, BUT THEY STILL PLAY A VITAL ROLE WHERE THEY ARE LOCATED.

If you are not sure if there is one nearby, you can easily call your city or search on the internet. There is an orphanage in my town and I am passing on easy ways to help. However, it is always best to learn more by calling, visiting, or reviewing the website for suggestions on how you can create an impact in their organization.

ORPHANAGES
Orphanages are less common these days, replaced with the foster care system. The remaining orphanages tend to be privately run and need assistance in various ways. Another part of this community that is commonly overlooked are

the children exiting the foster care system when they turn eighteen or twenty-one, depending on the state's law, and without support can end up living in a homeless shelter. Recently, I learned about a couple organizations that address this very matter, one called a Sense of Home in California and Aging Out Institute based in Pennsylvania. Their websites are listed in the appendix. See how your talents and skills can help make a difference.

COMMUNITY CENTERS

Community centers are public locations where members of a community gather for group activities, social support, public information, and other purposes. When I went to learn more about my community, I realized that not every community has a community center. They can be confused with a government office providing programs and other amenities for its community. If you have a community center near you that is actively involved in enhancing the surrounding area, reach out and give them a call to learn how you can be a part of their efforts.

1. Volunteer to help with activities.

2. Advocate to add a new program that you are willing to start and oversee, such as planting a community garden or building a book or reading area.

3. If you are handy, help with any maintenance that may need your expertise.

4. Become a Homework Helper.

5. Join the Big Siblings—Teens working with younger children after school, doing homework, playing games, etc.

6. Donate household belongings for programs needing them.

IDEA INCUBATOR

SHARE POT

THE GLOBAL VILLAGE

ALL THE COUNTRIES OF THE WORLD COMPRISE THE WHOLE OF LIFE ON THIS EARTH. SPREAD UNITY AND KINDNESS.

1. Purchase fair trade products.

2. Purchase from companies practicing and enforcing fair labor standards.

3. Purchase from companies utilizing sustainable practices.

4. Find local chapters of organizations in your community that work on a global level and participate as you can.

5. Volunteer and participate in groups that travel and directly help communities in need. Make it

your family vacation. This can have zero associated costs, but it may involve fund-raising.

6. Give a gift of giving to a hard-to-buy-for friend or relative. Purchase a meal or an animal for a family in a Third World country.

Begin with your grassroots community, grow it further to your country, then take it one step further to help globally. It's impossible to overstate the importance of reaching out in your community and the equal importance of reaching out in your country. Doing so helps foster the strength to go one step further into other countries around the world, countries that need assistance to strengthen their own communities, thus fostering peace, love, and care throughout the whole world. Many organizations work toward this goal every day and offer countless ways you can get involved. Here is a great place to start.

Ruth and Charles volunteered for many years through Alfalit International, Inc., teaching nutrition, gardening, and solar cooking. They have been able to contribute on four different continents as a part of Alfalit's literacy program. They taught the community how to utilize what food they have in order to gain its fullest nutritional benefits. A community in Peru had an overabundance of a beet crop but was short on other foods. In order not to waste them, Ruth and Charles showed the people how best to use the beets for eating and juicing, mixing them with other juices, using the leaves as a vegetable of fried cakes, and making a dessert from the juice. The children loved the beet leaves, thinking it was meat, and asked for more. In another South American country, they taught the locals to utilize the peels of green plantains to add nourishment to stews. When the family appeared to like the dish, the mothers shared the "secret" ingredient. The families were surprised to learn that they were eating what they used to discard, and the mothers were quick to point out that the family said they loved it. The gift of teaching a skill will yield gifts for the students and the community for years to come.

IDEA INCUBATOR

SHARE POT

Summary

It starts with each one of us. A person's time is a valuable asset. When we use it to make a difference in another person's life, it has an impact. When many people start doing small acts of kindness, it creates a larger impact.

We seem to live in a daunting world nowadays and can feel that no one person's small action can make a difference. But I believe that every thought and action of ours has an effect in our world, be it good, bad, or indifferent. No one is expecting you to be the solution. I am asking you to be a part of the solution. A person who makes a conscious choice to participate every day in a positive way, sometimes as simply as helping another person smile, is part of the solution.

It is you, me, the individual, who creates change one step at a time. Our collective efforts create even larger positive change. Look around; you can find messages and opportunity everywhere today supporting abundance, happiness, and empowerment of yourself and others. If you are one of the many who works every day toward these goals, please share your stories to uplift and encourage others. If you desire to make a difference but do not know how, it is the intent of this book to be a tool to help you take the steps to reach out, even on the smallest level. We all need to start somewhere and then continue to build on it.

Be a part of the solution by empowering yourself and those around you with your thoughts and actions filled with love and support. The more people working toward this goal, the more positive change we can bring into this world. We attract more of what we feel inside and share with the world.

Let's build on the many ways to make a difference and create volumes of stories about how we have contributed to the greater good of ourselves, our families, our communities, country, and the world. Pay it forward and share this book.

Share your stories and your ideas of what you did to be a part of the solution. We can do it. We can create a world of abundance, happiness, and peace—one story at a time.

Here are several ways you can spread the goodness of your stories or create ideas to help you keep your inspiration moving:

1. Facebook: Heart To Hands Movement community page

2. Twitter account: @HeartToHandsMovement

3. Instagram: HeartToHandsMovement

4. Go to the Facebook address listed above and post what you have done using the Heart To Hands Community picture frames and share what you are doing in a community and learn more about others participation.

5. Add: #Hearttohands to the social media posts where you are helping others.

6. Go to our website HeartToHandsMovement.com and learn how you can pay it forward with a Heart To Hands Tree project and book for a classroom.

7. Heart to Hand Tree Project can be given as gifts, used with your family, or even be a volunteer project at work.

Remember, this is only a starting point.
Adding other communities not mentioned in this book
will expand it's reach!

ALL MY LOVE,
~KATHLEEN FRANTZ

Appendix

A helpful start to learning about organizations that serve locally, nationally, and globally.

- Direct Relief—directrelief.org
- Map International—map.org
- The Rotary Foundation—samaritanspurse.org
- Samaritan's Purse—samaritanspurse.org
- AmeriCares—americares.org
- Aging Out Institute—agingoutinstitute.org
- A Sense of Home—asenseofhome.org
- Catholic Medical Mission Board—caringvoice.org
- United Nations Foundation—unfoundation.org
- Natural Resources Defense Council (NDRC)—nrdc.org
- Serve Your World—serveyourworld.com
- Volunteer Abroad—goabroad.com
- The International Volunteer Programs Association (IVPA)—volunteerinternational.org
- Alfalit—english.alfalit.org
- A Caring Voice—caringvoice.org
- Appalachia Service Project—asphome.org
- Young Neighbors in Action—cmdnet.org

Acknowledgments

I would like to thank the following people for sharing their stories and for helping to further expand the world we all live in. I look forward to watching the list of communities and ways we give back grow. I am truly grateful to live in a place that embraces community and making a difference.

First and foremost, my first grade teacher, Mrs. Parzack,
who I am confident has been watching over this project.

My children, who have supported me through many ups and downs
and choose to live a life that includes giving back to society
in a positive way.

Linda, for her friendship, volunteering role model
and supporting me in countless ways over the years.
Susan, who has provided help and assistance
to complete the final touches of the book.

My parents, my siblings, my friends, and my community,
for helping me to mold into who I am today.
A special thank you to Carole.
She has been instrumental in broadening my perspective in life
and strengthening my spiritual world.
Words will never be nearly enough to express my gratitude.

Finally, I would like to thank the many hands who contributed by sharing information about their communities:

OLD ST. PATRICK'S
Elizabeth (Beth) Marek
Director of Outreach
oldstpats.org

CORNER HEALTH CENTER
Kathryn B Fessler, MD PhD
Medical Director
cornerhealth.org

ANIMAL CARE LEAGUE
Tom Van Winkle
Executive Director
animalcareleague.org

JESSE BROWN VA HOSPITAL
Patrick Gleason
Chief of Volunteer Services
chicago.va.gov

THE FRANCES XAVIER WARD SCHOOL
Julie Johnson
fxw.org

FRANCISCAN OUTREACH ASSOCIATION
Diana J. Faust, S.F.O.
Executive Director
franoutreach.org

FRANCISCAN OUTREACH ASSOCIATION
Christine Curran
Director of Mission
franoutreach.org

UNIVERSITY OF CHICAGO MEDICAL CENTER
Sherry Iverson
Manager of Volunteer and Guest Services
uchicago.edu

SUNRISE SENIOR CENTERS
Lesley Durkan
Executive Director
sunriseseniorliving.com

ONLINE RESEARCH RESOURCES
theatlantic.com
philanthropyroundtable.org
philanthropydaily.com
nptrust.org
cafonline.org
nccs-data.urban.org

About the Author

KATHLEEN FRANTZ has a strong passion for spreading love and kindness within community. During her nearly thirty years in the culinary field, she studied under the first certified master chef in the USA. Milos Cihelka, and at Ecole L'Notre in France. At the same time, she raised two children as a single parent. Her main objective was to send them into the world with good heads on their shoulders, contributing to society in a positive way. She sought to integrate into their lives the foundational values of family within community and being a person for others. To support them, she used her culinary training to teach cooking classes, develop recipes for global food companies, edit cookbooks, and create comprehensive food design programs. Her passion for the culinary arts and community led her to found a certified woman-owned company, Katy's Goodness, focused on healthy snacks that give back to the community.

Today, Kathleen's passion for strengthening communities has blossomed. She is a member of her church's choir, she loves hosting dinners, and continues to develop her business. Now she wants to share her journey and the journeys of others to show the importance of unity within community. True to her passion, Kathleen continues to spread the goodness.